The Story of
BILLY THE KID

LINDSEY LOWE

T0054322

Enslow
PUBLISHING

Published in 2024 by Enslow Publishing, LLC
2544 Clinton Street
Buffalo, NY 14224

Copyright © 2023 Brown Bear Books Ltd

Portions of this work were originally authored by Tim Cooke and published as *Billy the Kid*.
All new material in this edition are authored by Lindsey Lowe.

Children's Publisher: Anne O'Daly
Design Manager: Keith Davis
Designer: Lynne Ross
Picture Manager: Sophie Mortimer

Manufactured in the United States of America

CPSIA compliance information: Batch #CSENS24: For further information contact
Enslow Publishing LLC, New York, New York at 1-800-398-2504.

Please visit our website, www.enslowpublishing.com. For a free color catalog of all our high-quality books,
call toll free 1-800-398-2504 or fax 1-877-980-4454.

Cataloging-in-Publication Data

Names: Lowe, Lindsey.
Title: The story of Billy the Kid / Lindsey Lowe.
Description: New York: Enslow Publishing, 2024. | Series: On the run: true stories of legendary outlaws |
Includes glossary and index.
Identifiers: ISBN 9781978536623 (pbk.) | ISBN 9781978536630 (library bound) | ISBN 9781978536647 (ebook)
Subjects: Billy, the Kid—Juvenile literature. | Outlaws—Southwest, New—Biography—Juvenile literature. |
Southwest, New—Biography—Juvenile literature.
Classification: LCC F786.B54C64 2024 | 364.15'52092—dc23

Picture Credits
Front Cover: Library of Congress.
Agricultural Research Service: 17; Alamy: Efrain Padro 26, Sheryl Savas 20, 27, The Print Collector 24;
Asagan: 41; Fineartamerica: 15; 38; Getty Images: UIG 13; Library of Congress: 6, 8, 16, 18, 22, 23, 25, 28, 30,
33, 42, 45; Mary Evans Picture Library: 4; NARA: 9, 10; Picturesque America: 5; Public Domain: fiddleStix 35;
Robert Hunt Library: 14, 21, 40, 44; Shutterstock: Matthew Benoit 12, Everett Historical 29, 34, 38, Jeffrey M.
Frank 19, George Allen Penton 37; Thinkstock: istockphoto 7, Sergejs Razvoovskis 31; Topfoto: Ronald Grant
Archive 43, The Granger Collection 11, 32, 36, 39.

All other artwork/maps Brown Bear Books

Find us on

CONTENTS

INTRODUCTION

Billy the Kid was famous in the West. As a gunfighter, he shot and killed more than 20 men. But he was popular with the ranchers he worked for, and with other people who knew him.

Billy's real name was William Henry McCarty. He was later also known as William H. Bonney. He is thought to have been born on November 23, 1859, and lived in the West at a time when there were few sheriffs. Many people carried guns to defend themselves or to hunt with. Even at a time when guns were common, Billy was famous for being a ruthless killer.

Here, hunters bring food back to a home on the frontier. Many settlers in the West lived in places where there were no laws.

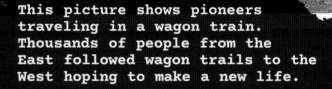

This picture shows pioneers traveling in a wagon train. Thousands of people from the East followed wagon trails to the West hoping to make a new life.

The Wild West

By 1840, nearly seven million Americans had moved from the East to settle west of the Appalachian Mountains. The land these settlers claimed had been occupied for centuries by Native Americans. There were many clashes between settlers and native tribes.

In 1846, the United States went to war with Mexico. After U.S. victory in 1848, American territory increased to include Mexican land in what is now California and the Southwest. When gold was found in California in 1849, the number of pioneers heading west quickly increased.

On the railroads

Some people headed west in the hopes of making a fortune. Others just wanted to claim land to farm. Large-scale westward expansion was made possible by the building of the railroads. By 1860, railroads spread a third of the way across the United States. The railroads carried settlers into the West. As the railroads grew, so did the number of small towns and settlements along the line.

Towns sprung up in a random way. They started with cabins made from adobe or logs. Then came larger houses and stores selling supplies. Services such as hotels and schools followed. Law and order was usually one of the last things to arrive. The U.S. Army had forts in important places, but huge areas were policed only by sheriffs.

Officials and railroad workers watch as the Central Pacific and Union Pacific railroads are joined on May 10, 1869. This completed the first transcontinental railroad across America.

Often, the new settlers were responsible for enforcing the law themselves. Disputes occurred when different people made a claim on the same piece of land. Ranchers wanted land to graze their herds out on the open range. They were angry when farmers began to fence off pieces of land. The disputes often ended in violent clashes. Some ranchers hired gunmen for protection. One of those gunmen was Billy the Kid.

Billy the Kid spent most of his life in New Mexico, living as a cowboy on the open range or in small towns.

Roots in Ireland

Billy's early life is a mystery. Although historians know some of the story, most of the facts are missing.

Historians think that Billy was born William Henry McCarty in New York City in 1859. His mother was an Irishwoman named Catherine McCarty. She moved with Billy and his brother, Joseph, to Indiana in around 1868. There is no record of Billy's father.

A devoted son

Billy was devoted to his mother. Catherine did people's laundry and sold food to make money. She sent her boys to school, so they learned to read and write. They later moved to Wichita, Kansas. In 1873 Catherine married William Antrim. By then she was sick with tuberculosis. The family moved again to the mining town of Silver City, New Mexico. They hoped the dry climate would help Catherine's health. However, a year later, Catherine was dead.

Some experts think this is a photograph of Billy when he was about 18 years old.

Billy was devastated by Catherine's death. His stepfather disappeared, and Billy and Joseph were looked after by a woman named Mrs. Truesdell. For the next year, Billy worked in Truesdell's hotel. He was just 15 years old. While working at the hotel, Billy befriended a thief known as Sombrero Jack. Many people think Billy's life of crime was the result of a bad choice of friends in his youth.

SOMBRERO JACK

Sombrero Jack got his nickname from the Mexican hat he wore. His real name was George Schaefer. When Jack robbed a Chinese laundry he got Billy to take the blame. It was Billy's first brush with the law.

Fort Wingate, New Mexico, is typical of the kind of small town that was scattered across the territory.

First Victim

Billy was jailed for the robbery at the Chinese laundry. But, he managed to escape from jail. He left New Mexico and headed for Arizona.

Over the next two years, Billy drifted around Arizona. In the spring of 1876, he stole a horse and headed for Fort Grant. In town, he took any work he could find as a cowboy or a cook. He also began gambling to raise money. When he had saved enough, he bought himself a revolver.

At Fort Grant, Billy met a local criminal named John Mackie. Mackie taught Billy how to steal horses. Billy became a skilled horse rustler. Soon, however, Mackie and Billy were caught. They were sent to jail, but Billy escaped again. He was famous throughout his life for his ability to get out of jail.

This photograph shows Fort Grant, Arizona, in about 1871.

These cattle rustlers wear masks to hide their faces in case they are recognized.

Death of Frank Cahill

Billy was quickly recaptured by the local blacksmith, Frank "Windy" Cahill. Cahill was a big man who had taken pleasure in bullying Billy. Billy was an easy target because of his slim build. Billy went back to prison but escaped again. In August 1877, Cahill attacked Billy for the last time. After pushing Billy to the floor, Cahill sat on him and began to hit him. Billy managed to draw his gun from its holster. He shot Cahill at close range. Cahill died the next day. Billy fled. He was now a wanted murderer and an outlaw.

NICKNAME

It was in Fort Grant that Billy started to be known as "the Kid." Most people think he was given the nickname because he looked so young. He was also short and slim, so he appeared younger than he was.

The Wild West

The American West was changing and gunfights were becoming rare. Still, its reputation for lawlessness was kept alive.

There were many myths about life in the Wild West. One popular story was that there was no law and order. It was said that people in the West settled all disputes using their guns.

Guns in the West

However, while most men in the West carried a gun, gunfights were rare. More often ranchers hired cowboys who knew how to use a gun in order to protect their valuable cattle from rustlers. Native Americans also continued to be a threat to settlers, who carried guns to protect themselves. If gunfights did take place, they were usually caused by disputes over land or family feuds.

By the 1870s, there were more sheriffs in the West. The enforcement of law was becoming more commonplace.

Many stories written about Billy the Kid had no connection with actual events in his life.

Stories about Billy the Kid

Frontier towns often passed laws banning the carrying of guns on the streets. The local sheriff could take their weapons. Despite such laws, many Americans still believed what they read about the West. Cheap dime novels were popular. They created the image of the West as a place without laws. After Billy became famous, stories about him appeared in many dime novels. They described him as a lone gunfighter. In fact, Billy spent most of his life as a cowboy working on the range.

COLT .45

The most popular gun in the West was the Colt .45 revolver. The gun was also called a six-shooter because its chamber held six bullets. The gun fit into a holster on the hip. The Colt .45 is sometimes called "the gun that won the West."

Cattle Rustler

Billy returned to Silver City, in New Mexico, after the murder of Frank Cahill. He soon joined a gang of rustlers.

Billy did not stay long in Silver City. He headed to the open range and survived with the help of Mexicans who were living there. Billy spoke good Spanish and was popular with local Hispanics wherever he went.

Joining "The Boys"

Billy joined a gang of rustlers known as "The Boys." They were led by Jesse Evans. Evans had worked for a well-known rancher named John Chisum, in Lincoln County. The Boys were one of the most active cattle-rustling gangs in New Mexico. They terrorized ranchers and local

This was the home of the rancher John Chisum in Lincoln County. Billy's gang stole Chisum's cattle.

Cowboys round up cattle on the range. The cattle herds were so big rustlers often stole cows without being noticed.

residents in Doña Ana County. When local lawmen began to catch up with them, the gang rode on to Lincoln County. There they began stealing Chisum's cattle.

Easy crime

Stealing cattle was illegal but it was easy because the large herds grazed on the open range. Armed cowboys did manage to stop some rustlers, but the gangs stole cattle under cover of night. It was often days before the theft was noticed. By then the cattle and the rustlers were long gone.

BILLY'S MANY NAMES

After joining "The Boys," Billy changed his name. He had been known as Billy Antrim, which was his stepfather's name.
Now he became William Bonney. Why he chose the name is not known. At different times, Billy went by Billy Antrim, Kid Antrim, William Bonney, and The Kid. He only became known as Billy the Kid toward the end of his life.

Raising cattle became big business in the West with the coming of the railroads. Railroads allowed cattle to be transported to the East.

Ranchers and their families lived in large, isolated homes. Their cowboys lived in a bunkhouse nearby.

Cattle ranching began in Texas in the 1820s. The ranches were run by Mexican cowboys known as *vaqueros*. In 1836, Texas became independent from Mexico. Texan ranchers drove out the Mexicans and kept the cattle. During the Civil War (1861–1865), the cattle roamed free and the herds grew. At the end of the war, the Texans rounded up the cattle and drove them north to sell. The railroads carried cattle to feed people in the cities of the East.

Expansion into New Mexico

John Simpson Chisum (1824–1884) was one of the first ranchers to send herds into New Mexico territory. He built up herds of around 100,000 cattle. They grazed on land he held by "right of discovery." This right allowed settlers to claim unoccupied land in the West. Chisum hired armed cowboys to protect his cattle from rustlers. When the cattle were ready for market, cowboys drove them north to the railroads. The railroads took the animals to railheads such as Chicago, where they were killed for beef.

COW TOWNS

Towns sprang up along the cattle trails that led to the railroads. These were called cow towns. They supplied the cowboys who drove the cattle. A typical cow town had places to sleep and eat. There were saloons where men drank and gambled away their earnings. A general store sold all kinds of supplies.

Modern cowboys still drive cattle across the range. Herds are a fraction of the size they once were.

Time Out

Around October 1877, Billy quit cattle rustling. However, it was not long before he returned to crime.

According to one story, Billy the Kid was on his own on the range when an Apache stole his horse. Native Americans sometimes ambushed white settlers and stole from them. Without his horse, Billy walked miles. He suffered from lack of food and water. He was close to death when he reached a farm owned by Heiskell Jones.

Barbara, Heiskell Jones' wife, was known for her good food and hospitality. The Joneses had a large family. They welcomed Billy into their home. Billy's stay at the Joneses' farm came at a good time. While he was there, the past caught up with Jesse Evans. The leader of "The Boys" was captured after a gun battle and put in the Lincoln County jail.

The Apache of New Mexico sometimes attacked the white settlers they found on their land.

Heiskell Jones and his family lived in the Pecos Valley of New Mexico.

Looking for work

Barbara Jones took care of Billy. When he recovered his health, the family gave him one of their horses. Billy went to look for work in Lincoln County. He rode into a tense situation. A friend of John Chisum wanted to start a ranch in Lincoln County. Chisum was backing him. However, local businessmen were determined to stop him.

LINCOLN COUNTY

Although Lincoln County was the same size as South Carolina, which had a population of some 700,000, it only had 2,000 residents. The main town was Lincoln City. Only 400 people lived there. The main street was lined with one-story, adobe-brick buildings. The town's only two-story building was the general store. The county jail opened in 1877. It was just a hole in the ground with a guard cabin.

Death of John Tunstall

In Lincoln County, Billy was soon up to his old tricks. But this time, his horse rustling had an unexpected result.

Much of Lincoln County was bleak, open territory. Huge areas were uninhabited.

Billy tried to steal horses from a rancher named John Tunstall. Tunstall was an Englishman who had moved to Lincoln County with his friend, an attorney named Alexander McSween. John Chisum had helped Tunstall buy a ranch. When Tunstall caught Billy stealing his horses, he did not send him to jail. Instead, he hired Billy to work for him.

Taking on Lincoln County

As a member of "The Boys," Billy had rustled cattle for a rancher named Jimmy Dolan. Dolan was part of a group of citizens known as "The

House." They ran Lincoln County as if they owned it. The House wanted Tunstall to leave town. Sheriff William Brady worked for The House. He sent a posse to Tunstall's ranch with a fake court order to seize his property.

On February 18, 1878, Tunstall and his men, including Billy the Kid, rode into town to challenge the court order. On the way they met Brady's posse. Tunstall was gunned down. His murder brought the feud with The House to a head. This was now war.

JOHN TUNSTALL
(1853–1878)

Born in England, John Tunstall wanted to make a fortune in the West. He used money given to him by his father, and by John Chisum, to become a rancher and merchant in Lincoln County. There he clashed with the largely Irish ranchers and merchants who ran the county. In the end, John Tunstall paid with his life.

John Tunstall was said to have been shot after he surrendered to three of Brady's deputies.

FOCUS Land Wars

Ranchers and farmers often came to blows in the struggle for land. The violent clashes were called land wars or range wars. The Lincoln County War was one of the most serious of these conflicts.

Much of the land in the West did not officially belong to anyone. Ranchers claimed huge areas, known as the range, for grazing their cattle. Cowboys were hired by ranchers to protect their livestock. In some places, ranchers argued about who owned the land. They sometimes fought off settlers who tried to start smallholdings or farms on the range. These settlers were legally entitled to claim the land to farm. But the ranchers were angry when the settlers fenced off parts of the range. There was less space for their herds to roam and grass for them to graze on.

Cowboys branding cattle on the open range. Ranchers wanted to keep the land for grazing. Farmers wanted to grow crops.

JOHNSON COUNTY WAR

In Johnson County, Wyoming, ranchers clashed with new settlers. In 1892, the ranchers hired around 50 gunmen. The gunmen invaded the county and killed opponents of the ranchers. The settlers and the local sheriff formed a posse of about 200 men. The two sides fought one another until the U.S. Cavalry finally ended the war in 1893.

This cowboy was photographed in 1888. Ranchers hired armed cowboys who used their guns to protect the herds.

Range wars

There were range wars in Johnson County, Wyoming, and Mason County, Texas. Dozens of people were killed. The ranchers could afford to hire cowboys, lawmen, and gunfighters. They behaved like private armies. The Lincoln County War was one of the most serious land wars. It was not just the ranchers and merchants who fought. Local lawmen took sides and the U.S. government had to send in the U.S. Cavalry.

The Regulators

After John Tunstall was killed, a posse was formed to catch his killers. Billy the Kid was one of its members.

John Tunstall's friend, Alexander McSween, wanted to catch Tunstall's killers. He tried to persuade the authorities in Lincoln County to investigate the murder. That would mean investigating "The House," the group led by Jimmy Dolan. However, The House controlled the sheriff. It was made clear there would be no investigation. Alexander McSween became scared for his own safety. He fled Lincoln County.

The posse

John Wilson was a local justice of the peace. He wanted to investigate Tunstall's murder and asked Dick Brewer, who was the foreman from Tunstall's ranch, to help.

This photograph shows three lawmen in Lincoln County around the time of the war.

Wilson gave Brewer warrants to make arrests. Brewer formed a posse known as the Regulators. It numbered up to 60 men, including Billy the Kid. The posse also included many Mexican Americans. They wanted to fight The House to end its control of the county.

Another murder

The Regulators spent five months in Lincoln County hunting down Tunstall's murderers. Billy was the most loyal of the Regulators. He was the only member who was present at every one of the Regulators' gunfights.

In March 1878, the Regulators tracked down Buck Morton, the man who had shot Tunstall. Three days later, Morton and two other men were found dead. However, Sheriff Brady still refused to arrest anyone else connected with Tunstall's murder. On April 1, 1878, six Regulators, including Billy the Kid, ambushed and killed Sheriff Brady on Lincoln's main street.

This is the most famous photograph of Billy the Kid. It was probably taken in around 1879.

The Battle of Lincoln

The shooting of Sheriff Brady triggered even more violence in Lincoln County. There were more deaths on both sides.

The Regulators met and fought with Brady's posse at Blazer's Mill on April 4, 1878. The Regulators' leader, Dick Brewer, was shot dead. He was replaced by Frank McNab. Meanwhile The House decided that the sheriff who had replaced Brady was too sympathetic to the Regulators. They forced him to resign and made George W. Peppin sheriff.

News of the violence had spread beyond Lincoln County. A unit of U.S. Cavalry arrived to enforce the law. They sided with Peppin and the men working for The House. The next battle took place in the town of Lincoln itself. The Regulators fought against Peppin's men and the U.S. Cavalry, but they were outnumbered. Billy and the Regulators fled to hide in the countryside. A posse was on their trail.

This painting shows Billy's friend, Tom O'Folliard. Tom rode with the Regulators.

Billy and the Regulators hid for weeks in the countryside around Lincoln.

The Five-Day War

Billy and the Regulators spent a few weeks in hiding. In July 1878, Billy and a few others returned to Alexander McSween's home in Lincoln. The House discovered they were there. Their men surrounded the building. For four days the two sides exchanged gunfire. On the fifth day, Peppin's men set McSween's home on fire. Inside, Billy came up with an escape plan. He and the others escaped through the back door. However, not everyone made it. McSween was shot dead as he tried to escape.

THE FEUD ENDS

The death of Alexander McSween marked the end of the feud between John Tunstall's supporters and The House. There was no point in carrying on the feud now that both men were dead. The House still ran Lincoln County.

No Amnesty

Billy became the leader of the Regulators after the escape from Lincoln. He was famous. But he was also a wanted outlaw.

The Lincoln County War ended with Alexander McSween's death. In just a few months, Billy had become famous. He was now the most wanted criminal in America's Southwest.

Peace offering

In September 1878, a new governor arrived in New Mexico. Lew Wallace had been an officer in the Civil War. To try to bring peace to Lincoln County, Wallace offered an amnesty to anyone who had been involved in the land war, as long as they had not been charged with a crime. Billy was already wanted for two murders, so he was not offered amnesty. Billy decided to try and get immunity another way. In February 1879, The House and the Regulators

Governor Lew Wallace was also a writer. He wrote the best-selling novel *Ben Hur* (1880).

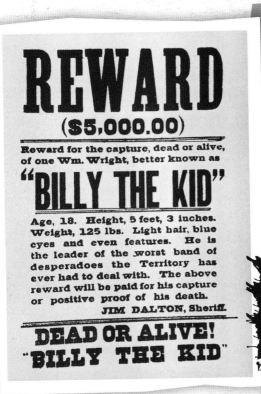

REWARD
($5,000.00)

Reward for the capture, dead or alive, of one Wm. Wright, better known as

"BILLY THE KID"

Age, 18. Height, 5 feet, 3 inches. Weight, 125 lbs. Light hair, blue eyes and even features. He is the leader of the worst band of desperadoes the Territory has ever had to deal with. The above reward will be paid for his capture or positive proof of his death.

JIM DALTON, Sheriff.

DEAD OR ALIVE!
"BILLY THE KID"

BILLY'S LETTER

Unlike many outlaws, Billy was able to read and write. He wrote a letter to Governor Lew Wallace. Billy offered to act as a witness against Jimmy Dolan. The letter shows that Billy was ready to stop the fighting.

This WANTED poster for Billy is a fake. It was created after Billy's death, when he had become famous.

met. They agreed to stop killing each other. They also agreed not to act as witnesses against each other in court. The agreement did not last long. While drunk, one of The House posse shot dead Huston Chapman, a lawyer who had been a supporter of the Regulators.

Plea for immunity

In March 1879, Billy wrote to Governor Wallace. He asked for immunity from prosecution in return for acting as a witness against Jimmy Dolan and other House members. Wallace agreed. Billy was put in jail while he waited to give his evidence. However, the government decided to put him on trial for Sheriff Brady's murder. Billy knew that he would not receive a fair trial so he escaped and went on the run again.

A Deadly Trick

Billy spent the rest of 1879 on the run, rustling cattle. In January 1880 he carried out one of his most famous killings.

Billy was living near Fort Sumner, a U.S. Army base in southeastern New Mexico. He rustled from John Chisum's herds. He said the rancher owed him for the time Billy had spent fighting on the side of Tunstall and Chisum during the Lincoln County War.

Famous story

In January 1880 Billy killed a man named Joe Grant in a saloon in Fort Sumner. The murder became one of the most famous episodes of

This is Fort Sumner. Billy ended up living near the small town that grew up next to the army base.

A revolver fires when the trigger is pulled and the hammer inside the gun falls against a bullet held in the cylinder.

Billy's life. Grant was drinking heavily. He boasted that he would kill Billy the Kid. He did not know that Billy was in the bar listening to him.

Empty chamber

As Grant became drunk, Billy asked if he could look at Grant's revolver. Billy secretly removed a bullet from the gun's cylinder. He rotated the cylinder so the hammer was above the empty chamber. Billy then revealed who he was to Grant and turned away. Grant reached for the gun and fired at Billy's back. The hammer fell on the empty chamber and so nothing happened. Billy then turned and shot Grant dead. It looked as though he had acted in self-defense.

MANY FRIENDS

Billy had lots of friends in Fort Sumner. He was popular with everyone because he was charming and funny. Many of his friends were local Mexican Americans. They particularly liked Billy because he could speak Spanish well.

FOCUS Gunfighters

Gunfighters are some of the most well-known characters of the Wild West. However, they are not romantic figures.

Billy the Kid was just one of the outlaws who became famous for his deadly skill with his gun. The buffalo hunter Bat Masterson and the Texan John Wesley Hardin were also feared gunfighters throughout the West. Other gunfighters became lawmen, such as Wild Bill Hickok and Wyatt Earp. These men were known for being quick to go for their guns. They were also good shots.

Western movies have created a misleading image of gunfighters. They suggest that gunfighters were romantic figures. They

The romantic idea of two gunfighters meeting in the street has been popular for over a century.

32

Modern Wild West reconstructions often include pretend gunfights.

show gunfights in which two enemies face each other on a dusty main street and race to pull out their guns. The loser ends up dead.

Disappearing gunmen

In reality, the real Wild West never had as many gunfighters as the fictionalized stories would seem to suggest. They only existed from the end of the Civil War in 1865 until the 1880s. Most gunfights were short and confused. The enemies rarely faced each other to draw their guns out in the open. Most were careful to take cover.

POLICE GAZETTE

The *Police Gazette* was a popular magazine. It told dramatic stories of crime. It started the myth of the gunfighter. The magazine told stories of the West that were read in saloons, barbershops, and pool halls. Each edition was passed from reader to reader until it fell apart. The accounts made gunfighters sound more romantic than they really were.

The Law Closes In

Billy's luck was about to run out. In November 1880, Pat Garrett became the sheriff of Lincoln County. He had fame and fortune on his mind.

Pat Garrett had been a bartender. He was elected sheriff because he promised to catch rustlers and outlaws, including Billy the Kid. Billy was wanted for his part in the Lincoln County War in 1878 and for three murders. Governor Wallace offered a $500 reward for anyone who could catch or kill him.

Wanted man

Pat Garrett wanted to collect the reward for Billy. He organized a posse and set out to track Billy down. He caught up with him at Fort Sumner. Billy was leading a gang that had been stealing horses. It was winter, and Billy managed to escape from Garrett's posse during a snowstorm.

This picture shows Billy shooting a man who had pointed a gun at him. The incident probably never happened.

Setting a trap

Garrett told people in Fort Sumner that his posse was turning back because of the snow. But this was a trap.

When the news reached Billy, he decided it was safe for the gang to return to Fort Sumner. They took refuge in an abandoned hospital building in the town. At around midnight on December 19, 1880, Pat Garrett's posse, which had been lying in wait, launched an attack on the hospital. A gunfight followed.

Billy's friend Tom O'Folliard was killed in the battle. Billy and some of the others got away. Yet again, Billy the Kid was on the run from the law.

Pat Garrett later claimed to be good friends with Billy. In fact, they hardly knew each other.

PAT GARRETT
(1850–1908)

Before he became sheriff of Lincoln County, Pat Garrett had a varied past. He had worked as a cowboy, buffalo hunter, trail driver, bartender, and hog raiser. He was said to have shot a fellow hunter dead in Texas. After that he left for New Mexico to open his own saloon.

Surrender

Billy blamed his eventual capture on the body of a dead horse. But he had already been betrayed by a trusted friend.

On the run, Billy and his gang hid at the ranch of a friend named Manuel Brazil. But Brazil betrayed Billy. He told Pat Garrett where the outlaws were hiding. Believing that Garrett was back in Fort Sumner, the gang had gone to an abandoned stone building. It was in a place named Stinking Springs, because the plants around it smelled bad. As the outlaws slept inside the hideout, Garrett and his posse surrounded the tiny, windowless building. Early in the morning, one of the outlaws stepped out through the door. He was wearing a sombrero, like Billy wore. No one could

This picture shows the dead horse blocking the doorway of the outlaws' hideout.

Garrett and his posse deliberately tempted Billy and his gang with the smells of campfire cooking.

see his face. The posse thought he was Billy and shot him dead. They also shot a horse. Its dead body fell across the door of the house and blocked it.

Surrounded

Garrett's posse settled down to wait for Billy to give himself up. Billy had a sense of humor. He and Garrett joked with one another. The posse cooked up breakfast and invited the outlaws to join them. At first the men inside the building refused to give themselves up. As they grew more hungry, the smell of food became too tempting. At sundown the gang came out of the house. Billy the Kid had surrendered. Garrett let the outlaws eat the meal before he arrested them.

A DEAD HORSE

A few days after his capture, Billy gave an interview. He told a newspaper reporter: "If it hadn't been for the dead horse in the doorway, I wouldn't be here today. I would have ridden out on my bay mare and taken my chances of escaping."

Jailbreak

After his surrender, Billy was taken to the small town of Mesilla, New Mexico. He was charged with the murder of Sheriff Brady.

Billy was put on trial on April 8, 1881. He was charged with murdering two men in Lincoln County: Sheriff Brady and another member of The House posse named Buckshot Roberts. After just one day, Billy was found guilty of killing Brady. Four days later, the judge sentenced him to hang on May 13, 1881. Billy was sent back to Lincoln for execution. He was put in shackles and locked in a room in the Lincoln courthouse.

Another escape

Billy did not plan to wait for his execution. A week after being put in jail, he escaped on April 28, 1881. Exactly how Billy

Billy shoots his guard, Deputy Bob Olinger. The two men knew one another and hated each other.

managed to get away is unclear, but he shot dead both his guards with a gun he got from somewhere. In some stories about the escape the gun was hidden in an outhouse. Billy then removed his shackles with an ax, stole a horse and some guns, and rode out of town. Billy's reputation as a notorious outlaw was sealed forever.

GUILTY!

Billy was one of six Regulators present when Sheriff Brady was shot. It is not even certain that he fired the fatal shot. But Billy was the only man to go on trial for the murder. In fact, he was the only person to be convicted of any crime committed in the Lincoln County War.

This is an illustration of Billy's escape. He later said he did not intend to kill the guards.

The Final Act

Once again Billy was on the run. He was now the most wanted man in America. His luck was about to run out.

Even though there was a bounty on his head, Billy did not travel far. His friends urged him to go to Mexico, where he would be safe from arrest. Instead, Billy returned to the Fort Sumner area. Three months after Billy's escape, Garrett and a three-man posse headed for Fort Sumner. At around midnight on July 14, 1881, Garrett and his men arrived in the town to look for Billy. Garrett asked around about the outlaw. He discovered that Billy was staying with a friend named Pete Maxwell.

This drawing of Billy's death shows Billy holding a gun. In fact, he was probably unarmed.

Garrett finally gets his man

Garrett also knew Maxwell, so he headed over to Maxwell's house. What happened next is not known for sure. In one story, Billy was in bed. In another story, he had just returned from visiting a girlfriend. Both stories agree that Billy went into Maxwell's room. He may or may not have been carrying a knife. He did not know Garrett was waiting for him in the dark. As Billy entered the room he called out "Quién es? Quién es?," Spanish for "Who is it? Who is it?" Garrett fired two bullets that killed the outlaw instantly. Billy the Kid was dead, aged just 21.

FUNERAL

Almost every citizen of Fort Sumner followed the wagon that carried Billy's coffin to the cemetery. Billy was buried alongside his two friends and fellow outlaws, Tom O'Folliard and Charlie Bowdre. Later a gravemarker was placed in the cemetery. The single stone is carved with the names of the three men and the word Pals.

This is Billy's gravemarker in Fort Sumner. There is a museum in town dedicated to Billy.

FOCUS Legacy

After Billy's death, his reputation as a heroic gunfighter grew. Some people even believed he had escaped and was still alive.

Billy's adventures were soon being featured in dime novels and popular magazines. The stories claimed to be true, but most of them were not. Within a year of Billy's death, five books about him had been published. One was by his killer, Pat Garrett. The books depicted Billy as a heartless gunfighter. They did not explain why Billy acted as he did. They did not mention Billy's loyalty to John Tunstall or how he helped to stand up against the power of The House in Lincoln County.

Dead or alive?

In the 1920s there was renewed interest in Billy's life and death. Since then, he has been the subject of many movies and books. Some of them claim that Billy the Kid escaped from the house

Pat Garrett's book about Billy the Kid was published in 1882.

The 1988 movie *Young Guns* told the story of Billy during the Lincoln County War. Historians praised the film's accuracy.

of Pete Maxwell. They argued that he was too good a gunman to be caught off guard. They say that Pat Garrett must really have shot another outlaw that night. Whoever Garrett shot is the man buried in Fort Sumner cemetery.

At least 20 men later claimed to be Billy the Kid. The two who appeared to have the strongest claims were John Miller and Ollie Roberts. To try to solve the mystery, a plan was made in 2004 to carry out DNA tests. The plan failed because no one knows which grave is Billy's. So it is still possible that Billy the Kid survived.

HERO IN NEW MEXICO

For the people of New Mexico, Billy remains a heroic figure. He helped stand up to the ranchers who ran Lincoln County. When it seemed Billy's body might be dug up in 2004, the governor of New Mexico hired a lawyer to represent Billy's interests.

Rogues' Gallery

Billy the Kid was not the only famous outlaw in the West. There were other rustlers and gunfighters on the law's most-wanted lists of the time.

Jesse Evans (1853–?)

Evans was a cowboy who was also a rustler. Evans recruited Billy the Kid into his gang known as "The Boys." He later went to work for Jimmy Dolan, which pitted him against Billy and the Regulators. Billy testified against Evans, who was sent to jail. There are no records of what happened to him after he served his sentence.

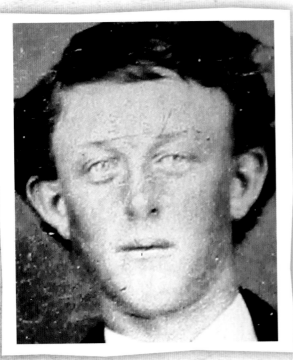

Tom O'Folliard (c.1858–1880)

Tom O'Folliard was a cowboy and rustler from Texas. He became Billy the Kid's best friend. They both rode with the Regulators in the Lincoln County War. O'Folliard was shot by Pat Garrett's posse at Fort Sumner on December 19, 1880. He died soon after.

Dave Rudabaugh
(1854–1886)

Dave Rudabaugh was a rustler who had been in gangs in Texas. He joined Billy the Kid's gang in New Mexico. He was arrested by Pat Garrett and sentenced to hang for shooting a deputy. He escaped but was later killed in an argument over a game of cards in Mexico.

Belle Star
(1848–1889)

Belle Star was known for her shooting and horse-riding skills and her great dress style. She was linked with the James-Younger gang. She is thought to have carried out a number of crimes but was only ever charged with horse theft. The crime was punishable by death. Instead, Belle spent nine months in jail.

Wild Bill Hickok
(1837–1876)

James Butler Hickok was raised in Illinois before he joined an antislavery gang in Kansas. During the Civil War he became a police detective in Missouri. Hickok became a town marshal but was also a gambler and gunfighter. In July 1865 he shot and killed a gambler named Davis Tutt in the first known "quick-draw" gunfight. He later shot and killed a number of men who drew guns on him. Hickok was shot dead as he played cards in Deadwood, South Dakota.

Glossary

Adobe Bricks Made from mud dried in the sun.

Amnesty An official pardon for a crime.

Bounty Money paid for capturing or killing a person or animal.

Branding The burning of an owner's identification mark on an animal's skin.

Court Order An official order made by a judge or court.

Cylinder The rotating part of a revolver that holds the bullets

Dime Novels Cheap, popular books that usually tell romantic or dramatic stories.

DNA A chemical that holds unique genetic information about a person.

Feuds Long and bitter quarrels between people.

Fictionalized Describes true stories to which details have been added to make them fiction.

Frontier The border area between settled land and the wilderness beyond.

Immunity A promise that someone will not be punished for a crime.

Pioneers The first people to settle a new region.

Posse A group of citizens helping a sheriff.

Railheads Towns where railroads join important roads or trails.

Range An open area of land where livestock can wander.

Revolver A pistol with a revolving chamber to hold bullets.

Reward Money Offered in return for the capture or killing of a wanted criminal.

Romantic Associated with an idealized view of reality.

Rustler Someone who steals cattle or horses.

Shackles Metal cuffs used to chain a prisoner's wrists or ankles together.

Sheriffs Officials whose job it is to enforce laws and arrest law-breakers.

Smallholding A small property used for farming.

Terrorized Caused someone to feel fear and terror.

Warrants Documents authorizing an arrest.

Further Resources

Books

Bearce, Stephanie. *Awesome, Disgusting, Unusual Facts about the Wild West*. Black Rabbit Books, 2024.

Captivating History. *Billy the Kid: A Captivating Guide to a Notorious Gunfighter of the American Old West and His Feud with Pat Garrett* . Captivating History, 2021.

Gardner, Mark Lee. *To Hell on a Fast Horse: The Untold Story of Billy the Kid and Pat Garrett*. Mariner Books, 2020.

Websites

www.eyewitnesstohistory.com/billythekid.htm
An eyewitness account of Billy's death written by his killer, Sheriff Pat Garrett.

www.pbs.org/wgbh/americanexperience/films/billy/#part01
A PBS page supporting the documentary *Billy the Kid*, with clips from the show and many links to background information.

www.biography.com/people/billy-the-kid-278971
Biography.com life of Billy the Kid, with many links.

www.historyhit.com/facts-about-billy-the-kid/
A page from the Historyhit website with 10 facts about the Wild West's most wanted outlaw.

INDEX

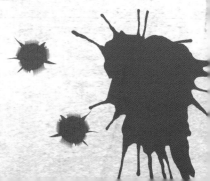